...tly
• Simple •

Chicken
turkey and duck

Marilyn Bright

ILLUSTRATED BY CONOR McLOUGHLIN

Appletree Press

First published in 1993 by
The Appletree Press Ltd,
19–21 Alfred Street, Belfast BT2 8DL
Tel. +44 232 243074 Fax +44 232 246756

Perfectly Simple: Chicken, Turkey and Duck

A catalogue record for this book is
available from The British Library.

ISBN 0-86281-389-1

9 8 7 6 5 4 3 2 1

Introduction

One of the earliest recorded recipes for chicken was set down by the Roman Apicius, who sauced the bird with dill, mint, dates, vinegar, mustard and fermented grape juice.

His recipe may seem a little extreme until we remember that the same elements are used to cook poultry today, with herbs and fruits, sweet and sour flavours and the mellowing influence of wine.

In this book, our recipes draw on earlier times and the cooking traditions of many countries – Italian-style chicken with flavourful tomato sauce, spicy Indian curry, Malaysian satay, sophisticated pheasant with cream and apples in the French style. Today's kitchens are culinary crossroads where foods of different cultures and ages can be tried and enjoyed. We hope that this little collection of recipes will be a valued guide to many gastronomic adventures.

A note on measures

Metric, imperial and volume measurements are given for all the recipes. For best results use one set only. Spoon measurements are level except where otherwise indicated. Seasonings can be adjusted to taste. Recipes are for four unless otherwise indicated.

Chicken with Forty Cloves of Garlic

In the Basque country, this classic French dish might be made with a pound or two of garlic. This more restrained version features the chicken liver combined with the garlic and chicken juices in a rich pâté to accompany the roast bird.

1 large 3¹/₂ – 4lb/1.5–1.8kg roasting chicken,
with its liver
bay leaf, sprigs of fresh parsley and thyme
salt, pepper
¹/₂ oz/15g/1 tbsp butter
1 tbsp olive oil
40 cloves garlic, peeled
6 thick slices French bread
(serves 6)

Pre-heat oven to gas mark 2, 300°F, 150°C. Clean chicken well, season inside and out with salt and pepper and place herbs in cavity. Heat butter and oil together and brown chicken quickly on all sides. Place chicken in ovenproof dish, surround with garlic cloves and cover tightly. Cook slowly in oven for about 2 hours or until chicken is very tender. Half an hour before the end of cooking, place chicken liver in dish to cook alongside garlic. To serve, remove chicken to a warm platter. Mash the cooked garlic, chicken liver and enough of the pan juices to form a pâté. Toast the bread slices, spread with the pâté and place around the chicken.

Tandoori Chicken

There are many commercial tandoori mixtures, but it is quite easy to blend your own, adjusting heat and spiciness to suit your taste. The brilliant scarlet colouring favoured in India can be achieved with a few drops of red and yellow food colouring, if wished.

3lb/1.5kg chicken pieces
1 medium onion, peeled and chopped
1 fresh chilli, de-seeded and chopped
2 in / 5 cm piece fresh root ginger, chopped
4 cloves garlic, peeled and chopped
3 tsp ground coriander
3 tsp ground cumin
2 tsp turmeric
1/2 tsp ground cinnamon
1/2 tsp ground black pepper
1/4 tsp ground cloves
8 fl oz/250ml/1 cup natural yoghurt
juice of 1 lemon
2 tbsp oil

Skin the chicken pieces and slash the thick fleshy parts. Combine the onion, chilli, ginger and garlic in a blender or food processor and blend to a fine paste. Add the other ingredients and mix well. Pour marinade over prepared chicken in a glass or ceramic dish and stir to coat evenly. Cover and refrigerate for several hours. Cook over charcoal or on a baking tray in a very hot oven at gas mark 8, 450°F, 230°C, turning frequently until cooked through, about 30 minutes.

Creamy Chicken Liver Pâté

This smooth spreadable pâté is quickly made, for serving with crusty French bread or buttered toast and piquant Cumberland sauce. If not to be used immediately, pack it into a dish, seal the top with a layer of melted butter and refrigerate for up to three days.

10oz/275g chicken livers
2 cloves garlic, peeled and crushed
sprig of thyme
4 tbsp/60ml/$^1/_3$ cup dry sherry
5oz/150g/$^2/_3$ cup butter
salt, black pepper

Carefully remove all membrane and discoloured parts from the chicken livers. Place in a frying pan with the garlic, thyme, sherry and half the butter. Cook over very gentle heat until livers are cooked through, but still tender. Discard garlic and thyme and liquidise the livers with their cooking liquid and the remaining butter in a blender or food processor. Season to taste with salt and pepper. Transfer to a bowl or individual serving dishes and chill until firm.

Poulet au Fromage

Chicken in Blue Cheese Sauce

Creamy cheese sauce masks gently poached chicken in a dish that looks professional, but is simple enough for novice cooks. For a special occasion, use all chicken breasts instead of quarters.

3lb/1.5kg roasting chicken, quartered
1 small onion, peeled and quartered
1 clove garlic, peeled and crushed
3 parsley stems
1 glass/6 fl oz/³/₄ cup dry white wine
4 fl oz/125ml/¹/₂ cup single cream
1 egg yolk
3oz/75g/¹/₂ cup blue cheese, crumbled
salt, pepper

Put chicken into deep frying pan with onion, garlic, parsley stems and wine. Add just enough water to half cover chicken. Cover and simmer gently until cooked through, about 50–60 minutes. Remove chicken to gratin dish and keep warm. Strain cooking liquid, return to high heat and reduce quickly to a scant ¹/₂ pint/300ml/1 cup. Reduce heat, stir in half the cream and stir until thickened. Beat egg yolk with remaining cream and stir slowly into sauce. Blend the cheese until smooth with a little of the sauce, then stir all together. Taste and season as necessary, then pour sauce over chicken in gratin dish. Put under hot grill until sauce is bubbling and golden.

Chicken and Almond Croquettes

Crispy coated morsels with creamy centres make good use of chicken bits for family meals or party snacks. Serve with spicy chutney or your favourite dip.

1oz/25g/1 tbsp butter
2 tbsp plain flour
6 fl oz/180ml/³/₄ cup milk
10oz/275g/2 cups cooked chicken meat, diced
1 egg, beaten
salt, pepper, pinch of freshly-grated nutmeg
4 tbsp dried breadcrumbs
4 tbsp chopped almonds
oil

Make a thick white sauce by melting the butter, stirring in flour and beating in milk over heat until sauce is smooth. Remove from heat and stir in chicken and egg, seasoning to taste with salt, pepper and nutmeg. Form chicken mixture into small patties or cork shapes and roll in the combined breadcrumbs and almonds. Fry until golden, drain on kitchen paper and serve hot.

Devilled Drumsticks

Piquant devilled chicken was the Victorian cook's favourite way of recycling leftovers as a lunchtime or supper treat. It is really too good to wait until there is leftover chicken!

8 chicken drumsticks, cooked
2oz/50g/4 tbsp butter, softened
1 tbsp English mustard
1 tbsp mango chutney
4 tbsp dried breadcrumbs
salt
pinch of cayenne pepper

Wrap drumsticks in foil and heat for 10 minutes in a moderate oven, gas mark 4, 350°F, 180°C. Mix together all the remaining ingredients; taste and adjust seasoning. Spread mixture over one side of drumsticks and grill under medium heat until just browned and crisp. Turn drumsticks over and repeat process on other side. Serve hot.

Turkey and Ham Risotto

The leftover treats of a holiday buffet take on new glamour when given the Italian treatment. Special Arborio rice is essential for the authentic creamy texture and your own freshly-grated Parmesan is far superior to the pre-processed sort.

1½ oz/40g/3 tbsp butter
1 small onion, peeled and finely chopped
12oz/350g/2 cups Arborio rice
1 glass/6 fl oz/¾ cup dry white wine
1¾ pt/1 ltr/4½ cups turkey or chicken stock
pinch of saffron strands (optional)
10oz/275g/2 cups cooked, diced turkey and ham
salt, pepper
freshly-grated Parmesan cheese

Melt butter and gently sauté onion and rice until onion is transparent. Pour in wine and stock, bring to the boil then lower heat and simmer for 20 minutes. Dissolve saffron in a small amount of water, if using, and add to the rice along with the turkey and ham. Cook for a further 10 minutes, adding more water if necessary. Season to taste with salt and pepper. Serve immediately with grated Parmesan handed separately.

Drunken Chicken

Subtle Eastern flavours and an unforgettable name distinguish this deceptively easy dish, perfect for a grand buffet or an elegant picnic.

1 large 3¹/₂–4lb/1.5–1.8kg roasting chicken
salt
4 spring onions, trimmed and split
4 thin slices fresh root ginger, peeled
5 tbsp light soy sauce
¹/₂ pt/300ml/1 cup rice wine or dry sherry
sliced spring onions for garnish
(serves 4–6)

Clean chicken well and rub with salt inside and out. Place onions and ginger in cavity and put into snug-fitting pot with the soy sauce and just enough water to cover. Bring to the boil, then cover and simmer for about 45 minutes or until cooked through. Remove from heat and allow to cool in cooking liquid. When cold, drain and bone chicken. Cut flesh into neat shapes and arrange in shallow dish discarding skin. Mix wine or sherry with an equal quantity of the cooking liquid and pour over the chicken in dish. Cover and refrigerate for 1–2 days, turning occasionally. Serve cold with sliced spring onions scattered over.

Lemon and Mint Chicken

The flavour combination may seem odd, but the lemon and mint bring out delicious Middle-Eastern nuances. This is a perfect summer dish for when the garden mint has run riot.

juice and grated rind of 1 lemon
1 clove garlic, peeled and crushed
2 tsp crushed cumin seeds
1 tsp turmeric
5 fl oz/150ml/²/₃ cup thick natural yoghurt
salt, cayenne pepper
3¹/₂lb/1.5kg roasting chicken, jointed
handful of fresh mint leaves, chopped
(serves 4–5)

Pre-heat oven to gas mark 4, 350°F, 180°C. Combine the lemon juice and rind, garlic, cumin, turmeric and yoghurt with salt and cayenne to taste. Place chicken pieces in shallow ovenproof dish and pour yoghurt marinade over, turning to coat pieces. Leave to marinate for 1–2 hours, then mix in mint leaves, cover and bake for about 1 hour or until cooked through. Remove cover during final half of cooking time if there seems to be a lot of cooking liquid.

Circassian Chicken

Walnuts, lemon juice and a hint of garlic combine in an exotic sauce with Mediterranean ancestry. A good party dish, it can be served hot or cold.

1 large 3½–4lb/1.5–1.8kg roasting chicken
1 large onion, peeled and quartered
2 cloves garlic, peeled and crushed
bouquet garni (bayleaf, thyme and
parsley tied together)
8oz/225g/1½ cups shelled walnuts
3 slices white bread, crusts removed
2 tbsp walnut oil
lemon juice
salt, pepper
paprika or chopped parsley for garnish
(serves 5–6)

Poach the chicken in a covered pot with just enough water to cover, with the onion, garlic and *bouquet garni* for about 1 hour. When cooked through remove chicken, cut into pieces, discarding skin, and place in shallow dish. Reduce stock in pot until it has a good concentrated flavour; remove *bouquet garni*. Make sauce by processing walnuts in a blender or food processor with bread in torn-up pieces and chicken stock to moisten. Add walnut oil, lemon juice, salt and pepper to taste. Process again, adding enough stock to make a sauce of good coating consistency, and pour over chicken. Garnish with sprinkling of paprika or chopped parsley.

Satay

Spicy aromas of chicken roasting over charcoal fill the air in Malaysian streets where hawkers ply their trade. Satay sold there is traditionally accompanied by hot-sweet peanut sauce.

12oz/350g boneless chicken meat
walnut-sized piece of creamed coconut block
1 tbsp lemon juice
1 clove garlic, peeled and crushed
$1/2$ in/1 cm piece of fresh root ginger,
peeled and finely crushed
2 tsp Chinese Five Spice powder
1 tsp granulated sugar

Cut chicken into small bite-size pieces and thread on to thin bamboo skewers. Make marinade by dissolving creamed coconut in a little boiling water and combining with remaining ingredients. Pour marinade over skewered chicken in a dish and leave for 1 hour, turning once. Grill over charcoal or under medium heat until meat is cooked through, turning frequently. Serve with a commercial satay sauce or simple home-made version combining crunchy peanut butter with lemon juice, a few drops of Tabasco and a little boiling water.

Coronation Chicken

This elegant dish with its whiff of the old Raj went out of fashion, but has happily been revived to grace modern tables. It is suitable for making in large quantities for parties.

🐇

1 large 4lb/1.8kg cooked chicken
1 tbsp oil
1 small onion, peeled and finely chopped
1 tbsp Madras curry powder
1 tbsp tomato purée
juice of 1 lemon
2 tbsp apricot chutney
5 fl oz/150ml/²/₃ cup mayonnaise
4 tbsp/¹/₃ cup thick natural yoghurt
salt, pepper
watercress for garnish
(serves 6–8)

Skin and bone chicken and dice into neat bite-size pieces. Heat oil in a small pan and sauté onion until transparent. Stir in curry powder and cook for a further minute, still stirring. Stir in remaining ingredients and toss chicken in the sauce. Chill and serve garnished with watercress.

Chicken in Champagne Jelly

Nothing could be more elegant than this chicken shimmering in its delicious jelly and wreathed in pale green grapes. If champagne seems a bit extravagant, medium dry white wine is nearly as good.

1 large 3½–4lb/1.5–1.8kg
    roasting chicken
2oz/50g/4 tbsp butter
1lb/450g chicken livers
1 large onion, peeled
    and chopped
2 sticks celery, trimmed,
    washed and chopped
5 smoked rindless bacon
    rashers, chopped
    salt, pepper

½ bottle champagne
1 small whole onion
bouquet garni (bayleaf,
    parsley and thyme
    tied together)
about 2 pts/1.2 ltr/5 cups
    light stock
powdered gelatine
small bunch of white
    grapes for garnish

(serves 6)

Clean chicken thoroughly inside and out and pat dry. Melt butter in a pan and cook livers, chopped onion, celery and bacon together. Season well with salt and pepper and allow to cool. Stuff body and neck end of chicken with liver mixture and secure openings well with skewers or cocktail sticks. Place in snug-fitting pot with champagne, whole onion with skin on (to give stock better colour), bouquet garni and enough stock to barely cover. Simmer for about 1 hour 20 minutes or until chicken is cooked through. Remove chicken and place breast down

in a tight-fitting dish. Reduce cooking stock by half, strain and correct seasoning.

Measure stock and add 1 teaspoon powdered gelatine for every ³/₄ pint/450ml/scant 2 cups of liquid. Stir over gentle heat until gelatine is completely dissolved, then pour over chicken in dish. Allow to set in refrigerator for at least 12 hours. Remove any fat from surface and turn out onto serving dish. Scrape away any cloudy jelly that may have settled on top of chicken and replace with extra chopped jelly from the bottom of the dish. Garnish with white grapes.

Honey Ginger Winglets

Easy to prepare, these Chinese-style morsels are economical and delicious as informal finger food.

12 chicken wings	*1 clove garlic, peeled*
2 tbsp clear honey	*and crushed*
1 tbsp soy sauce	*¹/₂ tsp ground ginger*
1 tbsp lemon juice	

Pre-heat oven to gas mark 4, 350°F, 180°C. Trim tips from wings and discard. Pierce meaty parts of wings all over with skewer or sharp fork. Combine remaining ingredients, pour over wings in a dish and leave to marinate for at least 1 hour, turning once or twice. Bake on a foil-lined tray until cooked through and nicely browned, about 30 minutes.

Cock-a-Leekie

A good boiling fowl, leeks and prunes are main ingredients for this famous Scottish "soup-stew". It pre-dates the 16th century and is still served at grand banquets as well as humbler meals.

1½lb/675g shin beef
1 large boiling fowl
1½lb/675g leeks, trimmed and washed
bouquet garni (bayleaf, parsley and
thyme tied together)
10oz/275g/1⅔ cups prunes, soaked
salt, pepper
(serves 8–10)

Cut beef into 2 inch/5 cm pieces and joint the boiling fowl. Place in a large pot of cold water, with half the leeks tied into a bundle and the *bouquet garni*. Bring to the boil, skim, then reduce heat and simmer until beef and chicken are tender, about 2 hours. Remove the bundle of leeks and the herbs and discard. Chop the remaining leeks and add to the pot, along with the prunes; simmer gently for a further 20 minutes. Season to taste with salt and a good pinch of pepper.

Pheasant with Cream and Apples

Normandy, with its fine orchards and dairying tradition, gives us this delicious way to cook a game bird, retaining its natural juices. Use the very best-flavoured dessert apples you can find.

butter for frying
1 large pheasant
6 large dessert apples, peeled, cored and sliced
ground cinnamon
8 fl oz/250ml/1 cup single cream
salt, pepper
2 tbsp Calvados or brandy

Pre-heat oven to gas mark 4, 350°F, 180°C. Heat a little butter in a pan and quickly brown the pheasant on all sides. Add more butter to the pan if necessary and fry the apple slices on both sides. Put half the apple slices in the bottom of a deep ovenproof dish. Dust lightly with cinnamon and put the pheasant on top, breast side down. Pour over half the cream, season lightly with salt and pepper and cover tightly. Cook in oven until pheasant is tender, 50–60 minutes. Remove pheasant to serving dish, carve and keep warm. Stir Calvados and remaining cream into cooking juices and re-heat with reserved apple slices. Place apple slices around the pheasant and pour sauce over.

Chicken and Artichoke Bake

This is a perfect dish for busy-day entertaining. It can be prepared early in the day, ready to bake when required.

2oz/50g/4 tbsp butter
1oz/25g/¹/₄ cup plain flour
8 fl oz/250ml/1 cup chicken stock
4 fl oz/125ml/¹/₂ cup milk
salt, pepper
small amount of butter
4oz/100g/1 cup fresh mushrooms, sliced
6 spring onions, trimmed and sliced
4 tbsp/60ml/¹/₃ cup dry sherry
10oz/275g/2 cups cooked chicken, diced
14oz can artichoke hearts, drained and halved
4 tbsp buttered breadcrumbs

Pre-heat oven to gas mark 3, 325°F, 160°C. Make sauce by heating the butter with the flour and slowly whisking in chicken stock and milk until mixture is smooth and thick. Season with salt and pepper. Melt a little butter and sauté the mushrooms and spring onions. Pour in sherry, cook for a further minute and remove from heat. In an ovenproof dish, layer the chicken and artichoke hearts with the mushroom mixture, then pour over the prepared sauce. Top with breadcrumbs and bake for about 30 minutes until golden and piping hot.

Chicken and Spinach Roulades

Pale green spirals of creamy spinach highlight an easy but impressive dish that makes its own sauce as it cooks. Preparation can be done early in the day.

4 chicken breast fillets
4 thin slices smoked ham
12oz/350g chopped frozen spinach, thawed
3oz/75g/scant $^1/_3$ cup cream cheese
salt, pepper
lemon juice
oil
1 glass/6 fl oz/$^3/_4$ cup dry white wine
8 fl oz/250ml/1 cup single cream

Pre-heat oven to gas mark 4, 350°F, 180°C. Beat chicken breasts out until flat and thin and top each with a slice of ham. Squeeze spinach very dry, then mix with cream cheese and season well with salt, pepper and lemon juice. Spread spinach mixture over each fillet, then roll up and secure with cocktail stick. Quickly brown chicken rolls in a little hot oil in a pan and remove to a small ovenproof dish. Pour wine and cream over, cover and bake until chicken is cooked through, about 20 minutes. Remove chicken, discard cocktail sticks and cut each roll into diagonal slices. Fan out on warm serving plates and spoon sauce over.

Chicken Koftas

These spicy little meatballs can be served as a first course or snack with dipping sauce made of thick natural yoghurt, finely-chopped spring onion and mint leaves.

8oz/225g boneless chicken meat
1 clove garlic, peeled
2oz/50g/1 cup dried breadcrumbs
1 egg, beaten
$1/2$ tsp ground cumin
salt, pepper
lemon juice
plain flour
oil

Put chicken meat and garlic through a mincer. Combine with breadcrumbs, egg and cumin, seasoning with salt, pepper and lemon juice. Form into 1 inch/2.5 cm balls and roll in flour. Fry meatballs in oil until golden brown and cooked through, about 4 minutes. Serve hot or cold.

Duck Breasts with Pears and Honey

The sweetness of fragrant honeyed pears together with tender duck breast makes a special meal. There can be great variations of cooking time required for certain breeds of duck and thickness of breast fillets, so check carefully during final cooking.

4 firm pears
butter for frying
lemon juice
salt, pepper
4 duck breast fillets, skinned
4 tbsp clear honey

Pre-heat oven to gas mark 5, 375°F, 190°C. Peel, core and slice the pears. Heat butter in a pan and quickly fry slices on both sides. Remove to roasting dish and sprinkle with lemon juice. Season duck breasts well with salt and pepper and brown quickly on both sides. Place on top of sliced pears in roasting dish, sprinkle with lemon juice and spoon honey over each. Cover dish and place in oven until cooked through, 20–30 minutes depending on size and type of duck. To serve, slice breasts diagonally, arrange on warm dish with pears and spoon pan juices over.

Chicken Baked in Salt

This Chinese cooking method requires a heavy ovenproof casserole with lid, just large enough to fit the chicken plus about 1 inch of space all round. The chicken will be succulent, tender and not overly salty if care is taken to dry the bird thoroughly before cooking.

3¹/₂lb/1.5kg roasting chicken
3 spring onions, trimmed and shredded
1 in/2.5cm piece of fresh root ginger, peeled
approx. 3lb/1.5kg coarse sea salt
(serves 5–6)

Clean chicken thoroughly inside and out and pat dry with kitchen paper. Hang overnight in a cool airy place to dry. This can be speeded up by hanging near a fan or moving air. When ready to cook, pre-heat oven to gas mark 6, 400°F, 200°C. Place the onions and ginger inside the chicken. Put a layer of salt in the casserole, place the chicken on top and pour salt around sides and over top to cover completely. Cover with tight-fitting lid and place in oven. After 20 minutes, reduce heat to gas mark 4, 350°F, 180°C, and bake for a further 40 minutes. To serve, knock off salt and cut chicken into bite-size pieces with a heavy cleaver.

Chicken Cacciatore

"Hunter style" chicken is an easy dish that cooks away gently without too much watching. It is even better made in advance and re-heated.

olive oil
8 chicken pieces
1 onion, peeled and chopped
1 clove garlic, peeled and chopped
1lb/450g tomatoes, skinned, seeded and chopped
8 fl oz/250ml/1 cup chicken stock
4 fl oz/125ml/¹/₂ cup red wine
1 tsp dried oregano
salt, pepper

Pre-heat oven to gas mark 3, 325°F, 160°C. Heat oil and brown chicken pieces on all sides. Remove chicken to ovenproof dish and sauté the onion and garlic together, then stir in remaining ingredients. Pour mixture over chicken in dish, cover and cook in oven until chicken is very tender, about 1 hour.

Steamed Chicken Pudding

Old fashioned steamed pudding is the right sort of hearty dish for the coldest days of winter.

⤿

Suet pastry:
8oz/225g/scant 2 cups plain flour
3 tsp baking powder
1 tsp salt
3oz/75g/scant $^2/_3$ cup shredded suet
Filling:
1lb/450g boneless chicken meat

6oz/175g bacon in one piece
2oz/50g/$^1/_2$ cup mushrooms, sliced
1 onion, peeled and finely chopped
1 tsp dried mixed herbs
1 tbsp chopped parsley
salt, pepper
4 tbsp water

(serves 5–6)

Mix pastry ingredients together with enough water to make a soft dough. Knead lightly on a floured surface, then roll two-thirds of the pastry into a circle to line a greased 2$^1/_2$ pint/1.5 litre/7 cups pudding basin. Cut chicken and bacon into 1 inch/2.5 cm dice, mix with remaining ingredients and place in lined basin. Roll remaining pastry to make lid, moisten edges and press edges to seal top and base. Cover with buttered greaseproof paper and foil, tying on securely with string. Boil pudding for 2$^1/_2$ hours on an old saucer or trivet in a large pan with water filled to halfway up sides of basin.

Chicken Soufflé Creams

Light, elegant starters like these can be a party piece for a cook who likes to show off.

6oz/175g chicken breast fillet
¹/₂ tsp lemon juice
2 eggs, separated
2 tbsp double cream
1 tbsp chopped parsley
salt, white pepper
(serves 8)

Pre-heat oven to gas mark 4, 350°F, 180°C. Chop the chicken meat very finely by hand, then liquidise in blender or food processor with the lemon juice. Gradually add the egg yolks, then the cream. Whisk egg whites to soft peaks and fold into mixture, along with parsley, using a metal spoon. Season with salt and pepper. Divide mixture among 8 deep, well-buttered ramekin dishes, filling no more than two-thirds full as the mixture will rise. Place ramekins on a baking tray and bake for 20 minutes. Serve immediately.

Duck Livers Escoffier

The great chef who made London's Savoy Hotel famous advocated the use of best quality ingredients, simply treated. This simple dish is a perfect example of his style.

10oz/275g duck livers
salt, pepper
plain flour
1 egg, beaten
1¹/₂ oz/40g/³/₄ cup very fine dried breadcrumbs
1 tbsp oil
¹/₂ oz/15g/1 tbsp butter
Cumberland sauce to serve

Cut duck livers lengthwise into slices, about ¹/₂ inch/1 cm thick or slightly less. Season with salt and pepper and dust lightly with flour. Dip slices into beaten egg, then into breadcrumbs, shaking off any excess. Heat oil and butter in a frying pan and gently sauté the livers, about 2 minutes on each side. Serve with Cumberland sauce or sauce made by heating redcurrant jelly with a little orange juice.

Brown Turkey Hash

Ordinary homely dishes are often the best, as in this Parisian version of hash, from a recipe first published around the turn of the century.

8oz/225g cooked turkey meat
2 medium potatoes, cooked
3 tbsp jellied stock
butter
1 small onion, peeled and finely chopped
salt, pepper
(serves 2)

Chop the cooked turkey very finely on a board. Peel and grate the potatoes, mix with the turkey and stock. Heat a little butter in a frying pan and sauté the onion. Stir onion into the turkey-and-potato mixture and season with salt and pepper. Heat a little more butter in the frying pan and put in the hash, pressing it into a cake shape with a wooden spoon. When it is nicely browned on the bottom, turn and brown the other side.

Chicken Curry

There are hundreds of curry seasonings, and regional variations from the Caribbean to the shores of the Ganges. This simple curry can be adjusted for heat and spiciness. Like all curries, it improves when made a day in advance and re-heated.

8 chicken portions
2 tbsp oil
3 medium onions, peeled and finely chopped
2 cloves garlic, peeled and finely chopped
2 tsp garam masala
1 tsp ground cumin
1 tsp chilli powder
1 tsp turmeric
salt
4 tbsp/60ml/¹/₄ cup natural yoghurt

Remove skin from chicken pieces. Heat oil in a pan and stir fry the onion and garlic until soft. Add the spices and salt and cook for a further minute or two. Stir in yoghurt and cook until mixture is a very dry paste. Add chicken pieces and fry in spice mixture, turning frequently until coated, then add water to barely cover. Simmer with lid on until chicken is tender and liquid is reduced to thick sauce, about 45 minutes.

Angel Hair Pasta with Chicken and Poppy Seeds

The thinnest variety of pasta may be labelled *capelli d'angelo*, *vermicelli*, *capellini* or *spaghettini* – all are suitable for this simple stylish first-course dish. Watch carefully as cooking time is very short.

9oz/250g angel hair pasta
2 chicken breast fillets
salt, pepper
1¹/₂ oz/40g/3 tbsp butter
1 tbsp lemon juice
1 tbsp black poppy seeds
chopped chives

Cook pasta according to directions, drain and keep warm. Slice chicken breasts finely, season with salt and pepper, and stir fry in a pan with a little of the butter until cooked through, about 3 minutes. Put chicken aside and keep warm. Add lemon juice and remaining butter to pan. Place over gentle heat and stir in warm pasta and poppy seeds. Heat for a minute then remove to warm plates, forming nest shapes. Place cooked chicken in centre and garnish with chives.

Index